Pioneer Women, Miners and Thieves

Golden Nuggets of History from the Great Arizona Outback

By
Cactus Kelli

Introduction by Sharon Rubin

Pioneer Women, Miners and Thieves
Copyright ©2008
All rights reserved.

ISBN 978-0-6151-9616-9
Publisher-The Great Arizona Outback
Rumor and Innuendo Historical Society
PO Box 844, Salome, Arizona 85348
gaohistory@earthlink.net

Original Copyright ©1990 (unpublished)
Treasures from the Mining Years

Without limiting the rights under copyright reserved above, no part of this publication may be reproduced, stored in or introduced into a retrieval system, or transmitted, in any form or by any means (electronic, mechanical, photocopying, recording or otherwise), without the prior written approval of the above publisher of this book.

The scanning, uploading, and distribution of this book via the Internet or via any other means without the permission of the publisher is illegal and punishable by law. Please purchase only authorized electronic editions and do not participate in or encourage electronic piracy of copyrighted materials. Your support of the author's rights is appreciated.

Dedicated to future generations of the
Great Arizona Outback

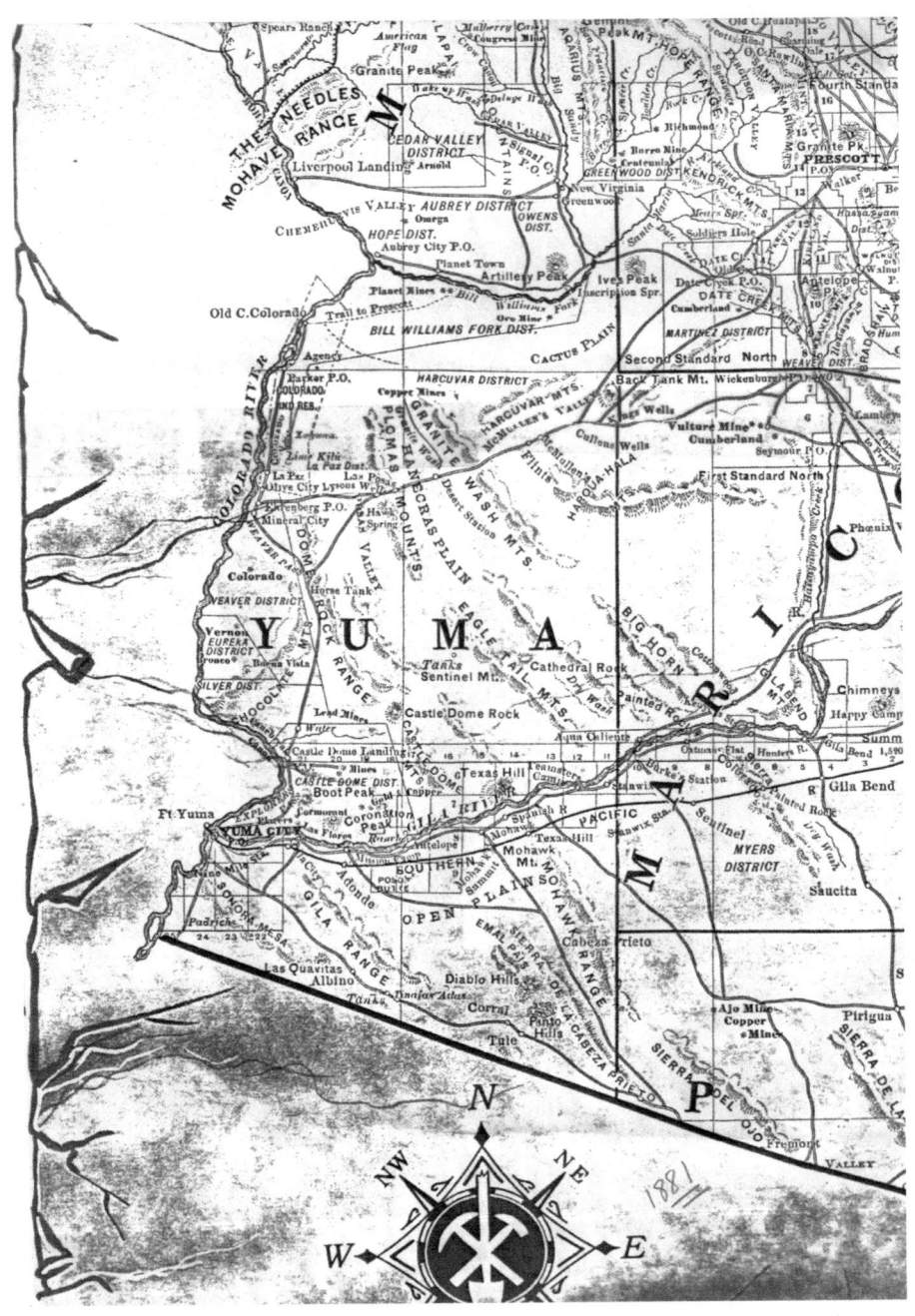

Old Map of Yuma County, Arizona.

Introduction

It was 1994, when I first drove through McMullen Valley. I was on a road trip with a friend from Vancouver, British Columbia. We had made our way through Glacier National Park, traversed "The Going to the Sun Road", and then continued in a zigzag path, so we could include Arches National Park, Monument Valley, the Grand Canyon and Sedona. It would be hard to imagine that we could be awed by more magnificence, but as we dropped down from Prescott into Butler Valley, then McMullen Valley, we were struck by the beauty and splendor of this fine desert. The dance of shadow and light on the gentle and welcoming valley walls - the green irrigated farm fields, mountains painted in different hues as the sun played hide and seek behind white, puffy clouds, in a very blue sky.

I did not know then that we had crossed over into La Paz County, a part of the Western Sonoran Desert, but I did know I had discovered a peaceful place.

About 10 years later my husband and I were making a similar pilgrimage to the Natural Wonders of the West. Heading out of California on the I-10, we got off at the Prescott/Wickenburg exit and continued along Highway 60 that mirrored an old stage route used by pioneer women, miners and thieves of a different century.

As we drove through Granite Wash Pass and came around the bend, past the petroglyphs, it was that time of day when the light paints the mountains surrounding our valley, different shades of purple, mauve and pink. I was awestruck. The view before me must have been the inspiration for the lyric in the song, "America the Beautiful". At some point, Irving Berlin must have also viewed the sun setting on the Harqha Hala Mountains, so he could describe their "purple mountains majesty".

Having come to live in McMullen Valley, I found myself speculating on an almost daily basis, who were the people who came here before me? What did they do? There are still fragments of another time, stone and adobe houses, old mines and just a few people left who can remember what our valley was like during an earlier time.

Cactus Kelli is one of these old timers, known in our community as, "the chronicler of our past." She has been a writer most of her adult life and has captured much of the lore of our valley in articles that have been published throughout her career in the *Wickenburg Sun, Arizona Republic, The Ribbit News* and *True West* magazine, to name a few. Although much of her writing is informed by extensive research, I most enjoy those trails she leads the reader on, that bring us to the stories of people. People that she either knew or heard tales about from other folks, whose lives in this valley extend back, beyond her over ninety years of personal experience. She may be a historian by avocation, but she is a poet at heart.

Cactus Kelli describes best what she attempts to give the reader when she says, "The tendency to sculpt memories is a natural phenomenon to soften the realities of our lives that are too painful to accept. Like the searing sun that can black out our sight, if we look directly at it, realities can sear our souls. But, memories are warm and comfortable and we all need them when we grow older. It is possible that I am one who has some favorite memories, but in my writing I try to present the realities of the past as I saw it. I have a dream of possibly being the last person to record a culture before it is lost forever; for more than two decades I conducted research in the archives from Sacramento to Tucson, about the land I have lived on most of my life." (Excerpt from an article in the *Wickenburg Sun*, 12/5/85)

I have been honored that Cactus Kelli has shared some of her stories with me and allowed a part of her work to be the first of, what we hope will be, many publications to emanate from The Great Arizona Outback Rumor and Innuendo Historical Society, named in celebration of the co-founder of Salome, humorist and satirist, Dick Wick Hall.

As editor, I have tried to do as little as possible, because it is her voice that resonates the truth of our history.

"In a movable culture such as ours is today, permanence may no longer be the necessity that it was to my generation. However, I cannot believe that we can sever a whole generation from our past, for somewhere behind the self we reveal to others, lies the backbone of our human heritage - all the way back to our beginning."
(Excerpt from an article in the *Wickenburg Sun*, 12/5/85)

Special thanks to my understanding husband, Don Eduardo, for his support and input, editing and patience, Phyllis Kriens, for transcribing the original manuscript, Linda Darland, for her help in preparing the manuscript for publication and the many angels of the Great Arizona Outback Rumor and Innuendo Historical Society.

Sharon Rubin, Founder
The Great Arizona Outback
Rumor and Innuendo Historical Society
February 29, 2008

Chapter One

Early Mining

In modern times, the coast of the peaceful ocean lays nearly three hundred miles to the west. To the south, the coast of the inland Gulf is almost as distant. Geologists believe that these two massive sources of water intermittently invaded the basins of southwestern Arizona until very late in the Cenozoic Era. Within the last three million years the forces of erosion, faulting and warping continued on a diminishing scale, opening waterways, so that drainage systems became progressively better. As trapped seawater receded, shaping of the present mountains and valleys gradually took place.[1]

At the same time, throughout the geological strata nature's pressure cooker was forming the precious metals that, after many millenniums, would become the earth's most valued minerals. Treasures so alluring, men (and some women) from around the world would be drawn to our distant valley.

Eighty miles northwest of Phoenix on Highway 60-70, McMullen Valley begins and stretches southwesterly for 48 miles. A shallow basin fifteen miles wide, bound on the north by the Harcuvar Mountains, on the south by the Harqua Hala and Little Harqua Hala

Mountains, and on the west by the Granite Wash Mountains.[2] The narrow valley lying between the southern slope of the Harqua Hala Mountains and the most southern extension of that range was called Harrisburg Valley. The rugged Harqua Hala Mountains in northeastern Yuma County,* rise abruptly from the desert floor like islands in the sky and is an excellent example of geologic landscaping.

An ephemeral stream known as the Centennial Wash courses in a semi-circle around the Harqua Hala Mountains and drains the entire area of McMullen and Harrisburg Valleys. In Territorial days,** the area was unofficially known as the Centennial District.[3]

The thirteen years between 1880 and 1893 were the most significant in gold mining history in Arizona. During the 1880's, a decline of commodity prices served to increase the relative value of the rocks that were discovered. An increased interest in prospecting for gold became uppermost in the minds of mining men.[4]

Rutted wagon roads penetrated much of the Centennial District, connecting it with most major towns in the Arizona Territory. Stages, supply wagons and travelers on horseback and wagons passed through the valley. Long before they arrived, clouds of dry dust, kicked up by

NOTE: * McMullen Valley was named for James McMullen, who was an early day stage driver on the La Paz-Yuma Road. The Arizona Miner, January 24, 1866, reported that McMullen had a hand dug well on the La Paz to Prescott road where he kept a first class station. He often prospected in the valley that is named for him.
This area is now located in La Paz County, which was formed in 1983.

** The Arizona Territory was created in 1863 as the civil war raged. Battles between union troops and confederate sympathizers across the reaches of the extensive New Mexico territory alarmed president Abraham Lincoln. In order to maintain a secure route to the union's gold rich state of California, Lincoln directed the Congress to establish Arizona as a separate entity.

animal hooves, announced their arrival. When a man became lonely, he could walk to the nearest stage station to visit. Prospectors explored the mountains and the Centennial District was no longer considered an isolated place.

Local residents visit with traveler just passing through.

In 1876, George A. Ellsworth came to the area for mining purposes and remained there to develop its resources. Ellsworth had first arrived in the Arizona Territory as a soldier in 1864, and was stationed at Fort Whipple near Prescott. Later he was sent to Walnut

Creek with other soldiers to raise livestock and provide protection against Indians for ranchers living in the area. When Ellsworth was released from the army, he continued ranching near Walnut Creek for several years before coming to the Centennial District. Eventually the District was renamed in Ellsworth's honor.[5]

A meeting of miners in Centennial District was called in early 1879. Ellsworth was appointed president of the group and C. T. Bancroft became secretary. Necessary resolutions, including the U. S. Mining Laws of 1872, were adopted and boundary lines were drawn for the first recorded mining district in the area. By that same year many mining monuments gave evidence of the people who had found ore in the district. The two most popular references used for identifying the site of claim locations were Centennial Wash and Mesquite Station.[6]

On September 26, 1879, the <u>Miner</u> reported: "George Ellsworth is up from Centennial, on the Ehrenberg Road, some 18 miles west of Cullen's* Station and reports the new gold discoveries in that section were nice…" A group of leads were said to have been discovered about four miles from Jesus Mungia's ranch. Large quantities of ore averaging over $100 to the ton were available. Safford and Company had reportedly purchased a ten stamp mill in San Francisco, which arrived in Yuma and was then shipped to Ehrenberg. Bancroft, from Wickenburg, was hired to haul the machinery to Centennial.

Note* The Historical Monument at the Well uses an alternate spelling, Culling, believed to be at the request of relatives.

The Oro Mining and Milling Company, a California corporation, purchased the mill. The ore mine was described as being in the Harqua Hala Mountains south of, and about equidistant between Centennial Well and Mesquite Station. The Oro Mining and Milling Company installed the first quartz mill near Centennial, with George Osborn as president and Edward K. Pope as secretary, recorded at the request of R. B. Safford.[7]

During 1880, location notices for mining claims in the Centennial District were using Ellsworth Mining District.[8] By February 2, 1880, a post office was available to accommodate the mining people in the Centennial District.[9]

Many names appeared on the location notices of mining claims in the Centennial area in 1879 and 1880. In addition to George Ellsworth, were William Beard, who was best known as Bill Bear, and John Rarick. Appearing on many location notices with John Rarick was the name of Carmelita Campbell, who was the first woman known to prospect and mine in the Centennial District.

Carmelita Campbell was of Mexican heritage. She married John C. Campbell, who became Arizona's delegate to Congress. While the couple lived in Prescott, Carmelita was credited with much of her husband's political success.[10] Yet, as Mr. Campbell rose through the ranks he took up with another woman, and Mrs. Campbell found herself suing him for alimony and the house she had lived in.[11]

Before the court ruled on her action, the "other woman" had Carmelita dragged into court, because she "feared for her life." The prosecution succeeded in convincing the judge the "other woman" was really in danger and levied a $500 fine against Mrs. Campbell.[12]

It was one year later, after her marriage to John G. Campbell was dissolved, that Mrs. Campbell began prospecting in the Centennial area. The earliest mine she and John Rarick located was the Carmelita Mine, on the south side of the Harqua Hala Mountain.[13] Today, almost a century later, the mine still bears the name Carmelita. The original location notice claimed all timber growing on and all water found within the claim.[14]

Mrs. Campbell worked the Carmelita Mine in the latter part of 1879, and early 1880's, when she had a camp on the Centennial Wash. Three arrastras were operated continuously. At one time she was reported to have had many Indians working for her. They packed ore from the mine down seven miles of trails to her ranch.[15]

Numerous newspaper articles between 1879, through the mid-1890's, attest to Mrs. Campbell's success in her mines. However, some men in whom she had placed her trust to do assessments and appropriately file proof of her claims proved to be Mrs. Campbell's undoing. In an undated letter M. M. Rice tells of her tragic later years. Rice, who claimed to have known Carmelita Campbell as a loving son would know his mother, wrote that a volume could be written about this pioneer woman, whose life had been filled with enough adventure, romance and tragedy to make her worthy of a place in the Arizona Hall of Fame. Rice said he had spent much time with her when she was prosperous and during the period of extreme poverty, when she lived in a crude stone cabin in Harqua Hala. In 1895, Mrs. Campbell wrote a letter to the <u>Sentinel</u>, reporting on a storm that swept through their small settlement on December 3. The storm arrived about midnight and rain came down in a sheet of water. In an incredibly brief time, a mighty rush of muddy water five feet high swept through the Wash, taking her house and many of her possessions. Several prospectors camping at her place lost everything they had. They barely had time to save their lives, climbing trees and clinging to them until the force of the flood subsided. She concluded, "I am not discouraged, as the mines are looking well…"

Centennial Wash flooded.

During her last days, some "so-called reputable citizens," stole her property and attempted to consign her to an insane asylum in Phoenix. They failed in their attempt but Carmelita Campbell was still taken to Los Angeles, where she died in forlorn loneliness.[16] And yet her presence in the historical record is evidence that despite her ups and downs, Carmelita Campbell was a force to be reckoned with, in the early days of the Arizona Territory.

Chapter Two

A Town Grows

In mid-July, 1886, H. E. Harris began moving machinery for a mill, from the old Sterling Mine near Prescott, to the Centennial District. Harris, along with William Beard and an ex-governor of the Arizona Territory named Frederick Tritle, had acquired many gold mining claims in the area.[17] The men anticipated turning a profit and expected to have the mill in operation within a short time.[18] The new town, located on the site of Centennial Well, was called Harrisburg, in honor of H. E. Harris.[19]

In September 1886, the Sentinel reported that Articles of Incorporation for the Harris Gold and Silver Mill and Mining Company had been filed in the Yuma County Recorder's Office. Incorporators of the new company included H. E. Harris, F. A. Tritle and William H. Beard.[20] It was reported the men were in the process of erecting a ten stamp mill at Harrisburg.

Before the end of September, men were employed taking ore from five different ledges, within a few miles of the mill. Water was plentiful around the mill-site at a depth of 14 to 25 feet. At one hand dug well, which was 25 feet deep, A. J. Law, the mining engineer, reported a steam pump, throwing 1,500 gallons of water a minute, had worked several hours and made no impression on the water-depth of the well. Enough dry wood from desert trees was readily available to keep a ten-stamp mill running for several years.[21]

Ore crushing began in December, with an abundance of ore on the dump at the mill-site and more being mined. The ore was reported to be yielding $35 in gold and $6 in silver to the ton.[22] By early 1887, thirty-six men were employed in the mines and twelve men were working at the mill. Other men were working for contractors in the hauling business. Some were moving ore from the mines to the mill, while other men supplied wood for the steam-operated machinery.[23]

On February 9, 1887, a post office opened in Harrisburg, with Mr. Beard as the first postmaster of the town that he helped establish.[24] The mail for Harrisburg came by way of Sentinel Station, near the Gila River. It was carried on horseback the intervening distance of 68 miles. Wes Bigbee drove the stage from Harrisburg to Phoenix in the 1800's. Phoenix was the supply center for the new town.[25]

Mexican laborers were hired to make adobe bricks, from which major business establishments and homes were built. The buildings constructed of adobe and lumber, were considered to be the most comfortable year-round dwellings in the desert. No air conditioning was available and fireplaces, or wood burning stoves were used for heat, as well as cooking.

In addition to site-built homes, Harrisburg also had tents, grass-thatched huts and other temporary dwellings, which appeared and

Typical Miners' Camp.

disappeared with the fluctuating population of the mining town.[26]

Twin look-alike buildings comprised the small shopping center in Harrisburg. One building housed the general store, the post office and stage office. Next to it was the saloon, with a homemade barber chair in it, for the convenience of its customers. The first barber chair was big and square with an old wagon brake arranged so the barber could control the angle of his client with one foot. By stepping on the wagon brake, the front legs of the chair were lifted from the floor, thus tipping his customer back for a shave. The headrest was a piece of board fastened to the back of the chair. The town also had an assay office and other business offices. A Chinese cook provided nourishing

Shopping Center in Harrisburg.

meals with the help of a kinsman, who raised garden vegetables, a mile or so southeast of town, along the wagon road to Phoenix. As families of workmen arrived, more adobe homes were built.

An adobe schoolhouse was built in Harrisburg. Not only did the one-room structure enable children to attend school, it also provided a place for community social affairs. Once the school opened, an occasional dance and special programs were held on Saturday nights. On Halloween, there were parties with apple bobbing contests and treats of fruit and homemade candy. Adventuresome young ladies came to the small mining towns as teachers. Wages were low and these young teachers lived as guests of the families whose children they taught.

Until 1907, when a legislative act prohibited it, gambling was wide open in the Arizona Territory, unless towns chose to reject it. "Girls" were also allowed in the saloons to assist clientele in purchasing drinks and to provide companionship. Girls received a rake-off on the drinks they encouraged men to buy. The gamblers and girls were both looked upon with tolerance in most mining camps.

In early days, water for household purposes was pulled from wells with a hand-windlass, poured into a bucket and carried into the homes. Laundry was done in round tubs on a washboard and homemade soap was used. The same tubs were used to bathe in. Most items of clothing were either made at home or ordered from catalogues. Even so, considering its remote location from a population center or rail transport, Harrisburg was as modern a mining town as could be found in the Arizona Territory.

Mexican families were a vital part of the population. Their children were needed to bring student enrollment to the level required to qualify for a school. The Mexican residents lived in their own settlement near the edge of town. Their dwellings had clean-swept yards and thatch-roofed porches, where families gathered in the heat of day during summer months. The Mexican women prepared paper-thin tortillas, baked on the hot iron sheet that served as a stove. On the back of the stove a large pot of frijoles would be kept simmering. The seasoning usually came from one of the blood red strands of shriveling peppers hanging to dry in the hot sun.

There was little love lost between Mexicans and whites.

Brawls sometimes broke out in the saloons and moved outside to interrupt the quietness of a desert evening. An interesting aspect of prejudice was observed among family pets, especially dogs. If a dog from the white section of town wandered into Mexican territory, it was attacked by the Mexican's dogs and soundly whipped. When the action was reversed, the dog from the Mexican residents' section suffered the same fate. No one was ever able to determine how the dogs arrived at what constituted their invisible boundary.

A few Indians lived in their own chosen camping grounds along the bank of Centennial Wash. The Indian women and their daughters washed clothes and worked at other household chores for Harrisburg housewives. When they were not working, they roamed the desert, constantly searching for seeds, barks and roots, from which much of their food supply was derived. On windy days they could be seen winnowing seeds from the dry pods of mesquite and other plants. Later, the pounding of rock striking rock could be heard, hour after hour, as the seeds were ground into coarse cereal or flour. For cereal, the coarsely ground seeds were boiled with water and honey. Sometimes little cakes were made from the flour and baked on the coals.[27] Medication and hair tonics were also made from various plant ingredients. The women also made beautiful woven baskets from willow twigs.[28]

Wood was the most important fuel for household or industrial use when Harrisburg was a town. Wood cutting and hauling was a profession that kept many men working. In the late 1800's, a cord of wood, chopped into desired length and delivered, cost between $2 and

$3. Even at that low cost, many families gathered their own wood. They pulled dry branches out from under dying trees and loaded them onto a wagon, or tied them on the backs of burros, to bring the wood home. Most men considered chopping wood their work, but it was not unusual to see an older son chopping wood. And if necessary, a pioneer woman could do quite as well as her men folk, when it came to breaking wood into desired length.

Coal oil lamps and lanterns, or tallow candles, provided lighting, both indoors and outdoors, in Harrisburg. Each day chimneys or "flues" on lamps and lanterns needed to be washed and polished. The coal oil containers on lamps and lanterns were necessarily small and they required frequent refilling.

There were no refrigerators or iceboxes for homes in mining camps. But, resourceful pioneers made desert coolers by tacking screen over a box, or specially constructed cooler, equipped with two or more shelves. The screen and solid top was covered snugly with several layers of gunnysacks. Only two other things were needed: the cooler had to have water dripping on top in adequate amounts to let it drip down the sides, keeping the sack wet, and it had to be placed in a shaded area where desert breezes could circulate. Many foods could be kept for reasonable lengths of time in the cooler, but meat was not one of them.

Beef was sold as soon as possible after it was dressed. Boarding houses, where food was served, were the best customers. With the balance of fresh meat, the seller went door to door to serve housewives. Any excess beef had to be processed into jerky. Jerky could be kept indefinitely in the dry desert air. Thin slices of the fresh meat were draped over lines and left in full sun to bake until very crisp. It was then stored in cheesecloth bags or white flour sacks and suspended from a rafter on a porch, or from the branch of a tree.

In the pastoral days of Harrisburg, many species of animals were plentiful around waterholes and in the desert. Game animals used to supplement beef included; deer, rabbit and sometimes burro. Dove and quail abounded in the desert from spring until fall. Predatory animals included coyote, fox, badger, desert bobcats, civet cats and many others. Occasionally, a mountain lion wandered into the lower desert from it's rocky home.

Eagles came down from their canyon-land lodge to prey on cottontail or jackrabbits, which frequented the brush thickets along the Centennial Wash. Great golden hawks wheeled and dipped against the brilliant skies and the red-tailed hawks haunted the loamy flats. Many smaller birds also flourished on the desert.

Nature held its own in those early days of pioneer settlement. The Valley was bountiful enough to support more than its small mining population. All it would take would be word of one rich vein and the McMullen Valley would soon become the destination for those eager to strike gold.

Chapter Three

The Great Bonanza

Long before the Harqua Hala gold mine was discovered, precious metal from "lost" mines were reportedly found in the Harqua Hala Mountains at varying intervals. In 1863, Henry Wickenburg and his two partners were searching for gold near Tenahatchipi Pass, when Wickenburg discovered the Vulture Mine. The discovery of gold in the "Hacquehila" Mountains was reported by a Pima Indian in 1869. The <u>Miner</u> carried an article on December 15, 1876, saying Indians had found new and rich gold diggings near McMullen Station on the Prescott and Ehrenberg Road. The <u>Globe Times</u>, dated November 1, 1902 recalling earlier times read, "...Little attention was paid to the (Centennial) Valley until 1876, when King Woolsey, George Monroe, and Dick Halstead...came across several hundred pounds of rich gold ore..."

No one has been able to prove exactly where the gold came from in the massive Harqua Hala range of mountains in western Arizona. A common experience among mining men in the Centennial District has been to find gold in almost unbelievably pure forms at times. Unfortunately, most of the discoveries were contained in small pockets of ore that soon petered out. However, there were exceptions. In the Centennial District, the most outstanding exception was the famous Harqua Hala Mine.

Even as the town of Harrisburg was being built, L. C. Shattuck of Bisbee, and his partner, worked a small placer in Harqua Hala Gulch near the southwestern end of the Little Harqua Hala Mountains, eight miles south of where Salome would eventually be located. In 1886 and 1887, the two men placered an ounce of gold each in daily mining.[29]

When Harrisburg was established, newspaper accounts of mining around the new town brought an influx of prospectors to the area. Among them were Harry Watton, Mike Sullivan and Robert Stein, who located several claims about six or seven miles southwest of Harrisburg, in the southern portion of the Harqua Hala Mountains. One day while prospecting on their properties, Sullivan found a nest of gold nuggets that he gathered up and carried back to camp in his hat. After checking location stakes, he found the rich ore was located on claims owned by Watton and Stein.[30]

For a day or two Sullivan searched his claims that joined those of Watton and Stein, but could find no gold. He considered various ways he might profit from his find. Finally, he approached the two prospectors and suggested the three of them merge their claims to become partners. Watton and Stein agreed and the partnership papers were drawn up. When they were signed and everything was in order, Sullivan brought out a hat full of nuggets and carefully divided them with his partners. When he showed them where the gold came from, they realized Sullivan had outsmarted them. They accepted him because there was little else they could do.[31]

Their investigation of the area revealed a blowout of gold so rich it didn't seem real. After gathering up the surface gold, Watton, Sullivan and Stein began mining and quarrying out the ore. By late 1889, exhaustion, incompatibility and enough gold to doubt much more would be found caused them to split up. They sold their interests that were soon after resold to A.G. Hubbard and G.W. Bower, of Phoenix. Hubbard and Bower installed a ten stamp mill. Within six months these men realized returns that amounted to far more than they had originally paid for the mine.[32]

The display of so much gold caused great excitement and another great gold rush began in the Centennial District. Many miners who had previously located claims and left, returned to pick up the mining claims they had deserted.

Harrisburg still had a plentiful water supply, and the Harqua Hala Mine purchased their water from there. The pumping plant was at the western edge of the town, which consisted of one boiler and two substantial pumps that operated day and night. Water was piped to a reservoir on a summit above the Harqua Hala Mine. From that point, water was distributed by gravity flow, through pipes to the Harqua Hala Mine and the camp. At that time Harrisburg's pumping capacity was 108,000 gallons in 24 hours. Because the mine operation consumed considerably more water than that daily, the tailings from the mill were caught on dams. When the water became reasonably clean it was pumped back to the mine to be used again.[33]

It did not take long for Harqua Hala to become a boomtown.

Town of Harqua Hala with mine in background.

Accommodations for workmen including a boarding house, sleeping quarters, and a general store sprang up overnight.

Early that year, Wyatt Earp arrived on the scene. The renowned gunslinger, retired and moving into a second career, brought everything required to open a saloon, including "girls" to assist the customers. He set up camp a mile out of town, as was then required by law. A post office was opened in Harqua Hala on March 5, 1891, with Horace E. Harris as the first postmaster.[34] Charlie Pickenback came to work as foreman. With a crew of Mexican laborers, the Harqua Hala Mine produced returns that amounted to 1.6 million dollars in a two-year period. One shipment of bullion alone was valued at $81,000.

Hubbard displayed the bullion in Phoenix, saying that it resulted from a 40-day mill run.[35]

Hubbard and Bower continued to operate the Harqua Hala gold mine until they sold it in June 1893, to a British company known as the Harqua Hala Mining Company, Limited. Before the year was out, the British company had made sweeping changes in the operation of the mine. Mexican miners were replaced with white men. By October 1893, Hubbard's foreman, Charley Pickenback, had been discharged.[36]

At the first Annual General Meeting of Shareholders, which was convened at Winchester House, Old Broad Street, London, on September 28, 1894, the Directors presented their first annual report and accounts for the period June 12, 1893 to June 30, 1894: As a result of active milling operations during a little more than eight months work, this first report revealed the bullion yield for the 249 days of operation was $291,336.90. Costs of production on the first report were shown as mining costs per ton: $2.61, moving costs per ton: $1.21, water supply, bullion transportation per ton: $0.22. The total production cost per ton was $4.04.

At this first meeting of the British firm, the mine still appeared to be making more than it spent, but it wasn't long until the Englishmen were having problems. During 1895, a 150-ton cyanide plant was built and the firm began processing tailings by the cyanide method. This cleared between $3 and $5 per ton. By the end of 1897, the ore body and tailings dump were both exhausted. While it operated, however, the mine produced between three and four million dollars in gold.[37]

With cyanide processing available, Harrisburg's business also picked up. Rich gold tailings that were residual from earlier milling of ore were recycled, and free milling gold ore continued to be brought in for processing.

In 1896, Harrisburg was still supplying water to Harqua Hala. The Socorro Mine had a company office in the town, and the saloon and boarding house were doing a good business. William S. Moffatt was operating the general store, and had been postmaster since 1891. The town had a butcher shop. Over one hundred men were employed in the District and that number was expected to increase.[38]

Chapter Four

Claim Jumpers

Among the many honest prospectors there have always been a few who practiced the art of getting as much as possible for as little as possible. In mining circles these men are called "claim jumpers" and the Valley had its share.

The 1872 Mining Laws required a prospector to make a discovery of mineral in place, before he located a mining claim. Monuments of stone were then placed at specified distances from the four-foot high post or monument that had to be built at the point of discovery.

Six monuments or posts were required, one at each of the corners, and one in the center of each end, parallel with the corner posts. A strip of land not more than 1,500 feet in length by 600 feet in width could be included in one claim location. A location notice required the signature of a witness in addition to a description of the claim, the name of the claim and the locator's name. One copy was placed in a Prince Albert tobacco can, which was anchored inside the discovery monument, and one copy had to be filed with the County Recorder's office within a 90-day period from the time of location.

To legally hold the claim the first year, a prospector needed to do original work consisting of a shaft eight feet deep, or an adit or complete a tunnel. In order to retain the claim, $100 in cash had to be spent or an equal amount of work done on the assessment each year. The work needed to be completed within a year, no later than midnight of the date on the original location notice. Failure to meet these requirements left the mining claim open for someone else.

A "claim jumper" watched and waited and a moment after the stroke of midnight jumped the claim by placing his own location notice in the Prince Albert tobacco can in place of the one it contained.

Harrisburg saloons did a land office business in the 1890's, while prospectors, many of them having met in other mining camps, partook of libations and did verbal justice to the necessity for assessment work. Much talking ensued and more than one prospector put his assessment work off too long, thereby losing his claim.

The story of one prospector whose claim was almost lost was that of a husky, good looking man called "Black" Henry. A name attributed to his black-whiskered face. Henry had a claim southeast of Harrisburg in the Harqua Hala Mountains, which he was sure required only a little work to open up a new bonanza. There were other men who thought Henry was right, and they stayed close to Harrisburg, ready to jump his claim if he failed to show up on time.[39]

Henry showed up in Harrisburg on Christmas Day with a full week to get assessment work started on his claim. He arrived with some cash in his pockets and started a celebration with an old friend, John Agard.

A tinhorn gambler called "Slippery" hovered in the vicinity. He had a covetous eye on Black Henry's claim. A few broken down prospectors and saloon bums hung around the gambler. As the evening went on and Henry showed no sign of sobering up, Slippery moved in and spent his own money to keep him intoxicated. Slippery knew none of the old timers would take advantage of Henry's drunkenness to jump his claim. He began to plan how he would get his own name in the tobacco tin.

John Agard joined into festivities with his friends, but he remained alert and never lost track of what was going on. He knew a man without scruples when he saw one, and he watched as Slippery went first to one and then to another saloon friend, talking to them in low tones. Quietly, John took a mutual friend of Henry's into his confidence and planned a surprise for Slippery.

John and his friend helped Henry off to bed earlier than usual on the night of December 30. The next morning they plied him with black coffee until he was his usual self before they clued him in on the scheme they had planned. Not only would the plan save Henry's claim, but they could also have fun doing it. All three men feigned drunkenness that night as they staggered noisily out of the saloon early, proclaiming in loud voices that they were going to get a bite to eat and then go to bed. In a short time they were all snoring loudly for the benefit of a spy Slippery sent to check on them.

Slippery rode out of Harrisburg shortly after 9 p.m. With his armed accomplices, he planned to put his own notice at Black Henry's monument. His men could be used to witness that the claim had lapsed because no assessment work had been done on it.

They arrived at the foot of the steep hill where Henry's claim lay. Leaving one man with the horses, the rest of them climbed the slope to the discovery shaft. Slippery struck a match and peered at his watch. It was only minutes until midnight of December 31. He looked down the slope. At the base of the hill he could see the horses in the clear starlit night. No sound of anyone approaching could be heard.

"Aw, fellows," he said, "nobody will get here by midnight. I'll just put my notice in that tobacco can right now."

Slippery stooped over and fumbled in the rocky monument until he found the tobacco can. He found the slip of paper in the can, and at that moment three men arose from behind a rock pile not more than ten feet away. With loud Indian yells, they began firing their six-shooters.

One bullet knocked the tobacco can from Slippery's hand another knocked his hat off. As the claim jumper and his friends fell over one another in their hasty retreat, bullets whizzed past their ears. Down the slope they ran, stumbling and falling over rocks and scrambling up again in their headlong flight. At the bottom of the hill they piled hastily into saddles and disappeared with a clatter of running hooves into the night.

Up at the discovery shaft three men had holstered their guns and were roaring with laughter. Finally John Agard managed to gasp, "Did you ever see men rip up the mountainside on their britches like that before? We could have killed every one of them if we'd wanted to!"

Chapter Five

Life at the San Marcos Mine

A lucid account of the daily trials and joys of family life at the San Marcos Mine in the Centennial District around the turn of the century is told by Mrs. John (Sadie) Martin in her manuscript <u>My Desert Memories</u>.[40]

Mrs. Martin's story begins with her arrival in the Arizona Territory in 1888, when her young husband, John Martin met her train in Sentinel. He had arrived to join his parents and two brothers five months earlier. The family lived near Agua Caliente, and eventually settled in the vicinity of Palomas near the Gila River where they ranched until 1897.

The ranch was located two miles from Palomas, on the road that led to the famous Harqua Hala Mine. Many travelers between the Centennial District and the town of Palomas, came by to get hay for their horses, and wagon freighters camped overnight on the ranch. The Martin family felt the excitement of mining from frequent contact with neighbors in the area. By 1895, they had become friends with many people from Harqua Hala. Wives often stayed at the ranch to visit with Mrs. Martin while their husbands continued to Palomas on business, and they often urged the Martin family to visit at Harqua Hala.

In the fall of 1896, Mr. and Mrs. John Martin, their two little girls, Gladys and Marcella, and a visitor from Iowa went to Harqua Hala. Of that trip Mrs. Martin wrote, "It was a long day's drive over desert roads. We arrived around dark and as we came up out of a wash, a beautiful sight met our eyes. Harqua Hala had the first light plant in the Centennial District and the camp was electrically lighted and the cyanide plant was a mass of brilliant lights. We were so splendidly entertained while there, it was hard to return to the ranch…"[41]

Gold fever had struck John Martin and his brother Rube. In 1897, the Palomas ranch was traded for a home in Los Angeles. Mrs. Martin and her daughters went to California to live in the new home with John's parents until he could provide a place for them to live. John now felt free to camp at some gold mining claims his older brother, Dr. Ancil Martin of Phoenix, had taken over. Rube and Sadie's brother, William Patch, went with John to help him work the mine.

The men pitched three large tents at the San Marcos Mine on the northwest slope of the Harqua Hala Mountains and went to work. The San Marcos Mine was located six miles in a northerly direction from Harrisburg, where mail and supplies were secured. Their water was hauled in barrels from Pete's Well, about six miles northwest of the mine. The only transportation in the Martin family for several years was a mule they called Barney.

Although Harqua Hala had a general store, saloon, boarding

house and school, Harrisburg was still a thriving town in 1898. The names of 39 men were entered in the Great Register of Yuma County, Arizona Territory for voting in 1898. Seven men were registered to vote from Harqua Hala. More than sixteen states and several foreign countries were represented among the population that year. Many men whose names appeared on the Register for 1898, remained in the area and took part in continuing the settlement of Northeastern Yuma County; Patrick and Martin Devine were associated with Alamo, on the Bill Williams River; John S. and Barney Quinn took part in mining; John Rarick and James F. Vickers also mined in the area; Jose Torres later operated a General Store in Wenden; Charles Dallman served as Postmaster at Harqua Hala in 1898; George Ward was living in an adobe cabin, on what later became the Nord ranch.

In the fall of 1899, the Martin family was reunited at the San Marcos Mine, which was now sometimes called Martin Camp. The camp still consisted of three large tents. One tent was used as a kitchen and dining room, another served as sleeping quarters for the Martin family and the third was where Rube and Will slept. A stone fireplace was built in one corner of each tent to provide warmth.

Mrs. Martin described their camp at San Marcos Mine: "Our camp was in a lovely spot on the side of a mountain and we could see many miles in three directions. If anyone was coming on the main road (the stage road between Congress and Harrisburg or Harqua Hala), we could see dust at least twenty miles away…the August sand storms would come rolling down the valley in great clouds and faster than a team (of horses) could travel, but we would just get the edge of

Martin Camp at San Marcos Mine.

it...we were never lonely. Someone came by nearly every day, and our friends, Mr. and Mrs. Barney Quinn, drove out from Harrisburg to see us from time to time. The water wagon came now twice a week..."[42]

A day at the San Marcos Mine began early in the morning. The men used Barney, the mule and a windlass, to hoist ore in leather buckets from the mineshaft to the surface. This job required most of the day. Down in the shaft, holes were then hand-drilled and dynamite set for blasting. The last job of the day was to set the fuses, strike them, and dash to safety, where each shot was counted aloud to assure all of them fired. During the night the resulting dust and debris settled, so that hoisting ore could be resumed the following morning. After the last shot had fired, the men returned to camp for supper. And in this way, the men worked persistently at the San Marcos Mine, day after day.

A surprising variety of foods were available to insure proper nourishment. There were always plenty of dry beans, jerky, canned vegetables and fruits, dried fruits, and staples for home baked bread or pastries. Occasionally, fresh meat and eggs could be purchased from local ranchers and were welcome additions to the meals.

Long quiet evenings were a time of sharing, sometimes through conversation, many times in thoughtful silence; occasionally Rube brought his banjo out of his tent and strummed a tune while they sang. The family carried chairs out to sit and watch the sunset fade into twilight. Stars seemed to move closer as the night grew dark, and in all of McMullen Valley the only visible light came from a window in the building at Pete's Well, six miles away.

The men took turns walking the twelve-mile round-trip to Harrisburg for the mail and supplies. When John's turn came, Mrs. Martin and the girls often went with him. Gladys and Marcella rode Barney, while Sadie and John walked. Many times, Mrs. Martin and the girls visited Mrs. Mary Reid, while Mr. Martin continued to Harrisburg.

The tent-homes became uncomfortable when heavy rain fell and moisture penetrated the canvas dwellings, but Mrs. Martin did not dwell on unpleasant experiences in her manuscript. She remembered with fondness the morning they were awakened by the sound of Rube and Will scraping snow from the tent. It had come in the night and floated down silently, to transform low desert plants into igloos. A blanket of white had settled over the mountains and valley as far as the eye could see.

One morning after a heavy rain, Sadie had taken all the bedding outside and spread it on lines to dry when Rube came in from Harrisburg with the schoolteacher. She had come to spend the weekend. Etiquette of the desert at that time was complete informality and visiting was a welcome activity. The schoolteacher was pleased to take part in family activities, which always assumed a party atmosphere with company. It was an occasion special enough for John Martin to prepare his favorite treat, which he called "Arizona frijoles."

He dug a pit and built a big fire in the bottom, using plenty of dry mesquite and ironwood. While the wood burned into a bed of coals, John prepared dry beans for cooking. He used a lard pail, with a tight fitting lid, for a cooking pot. The beans, with seasonings of salt, spices, and sometimes ground jerky, were placed in the pail with enough water to keep the ingredients steaming. After securing the lid the pail was lowered into the pit of coals, covered, and then filled with the soil he had excavated. Several hours later a pail of delicately seasoned beans, cooked to perfection, was removed from the pit. While the beans were steaming, John prepared dried fruit pies for dessert.

One hot August morning in 1900, an agitated Mexican man rode into camp on his horse. He asked for a container of water and waited nervously while John prepared a lard pail of water for him. He took it quickly, muttered, "gracias" and galloped toward the western mountains. A few hours later, a posse looking for a lone Mexican man, rode by Martin Camp to warn them a murderer was at large. William Moffatt had been murdered in the night as he slept on the porch in front of his general store in Harrisburg. One blow to the head with a steel drill had caused Moffatt's death. Only the bag of gold dust from beneath his pillow was taken. John told the posse about the early morning visitor, and the men left. They caught up with the guilty man at Desert Station.

Shortly after the murder of Moffatt in 1900, Laura Lamson, who was a friend of the Martins, came to the San Marcos Mine for a visit. Laura wrote of her memories in her manuscript entitled, <u>A Visit to Martin Camp</u>,[43] which she wrote at the request of Sadie E. Martin in 1939. Her memoir begins with a memorable journey on a freight train from Iron Springs (near Prescott) to Congress Junction.

Laura had intended to go to the town of Congress to arrange for her stage trip to Pete's Well. However, the train left her off in Congress Junction, four miles from the town of Congress. She had to wait at a small hotel beside the road until the local stage came to meet the passenger train at one o'clock on Monday morning. A number of passengers arrived on the train, and she boarded the stage with them.

Congress was very dark when they arrived in front of the Post Office. All of the passengers got off the stage and disappeared into the night. The Mexican driver went into the Post Office to sort mail, while Laura paced the dark porch of the big frame building. After a time, the driver emerged. They boarded the United States mail stage, an old spring wagon with a canvas top and side curtains, to move out into the darkness of the narrow dirt road that led from Congress to Harrisburg and Harqua Hala.

The small pistol a solicitous friend had insisted Laura carry in her bag, was of little comfort to her as she perched on the front seat beside the silent Mexican man. They bumped along the old wagon road into the lonely desert for more than an hour with only the creaking of the stage and the lively clop-clop of the two horses breaking the pre-dawn silence. They met two men traveling in a buckboard in the opposite direction, and at dawn they saw a sheepherder starting out from his solitary camp with his sheep.

The sun rose, and the day quickly became warm and bright. Ahead of them Laura could see endless miles of the dirt road stretching out across greasewood flats. The driver stopped the stage once to give the horses a drink of water from the keg tied to one side of the wagon. He handed Laura one of his tortillas for breakfast. While she nibbled on it, the man demonstrated how to drink water from his canteen and offered it to her. They started out again.

The hours dragged. There were no buildings along the road, no power poles, no telephone, not even a restroom until they reached Cullen's Well, a short time before noon. Laura described Cullen's place as having one small building where miners came from distant hills, to sit and talk and pick up mail. She filled her lard pail with fresh water at the well, and asked the driver if she could sit on the back seat to nap. He obligingly made a place for her. They began the trip to Pete's Well, and Laura leaned against a large roll of bedding to sleep.

Much later Laura awoke to find the Mexican driver asleep on the front seat, and the horses ambling along at a lazy walk. She made a loud noise. The driver quickly sat upright and urged the horses into a brisk trot. Whirlwinds twisted high into the sky across the desert floor. Far across the valley, lavender tinted mountains dozed in the brilliant sunshine of August.

Pete Nevarez.

It was late afternoon when they reached Pete's Well, which consisted of a building, a corral with horses in it, and a little green garden completely surrounded with ocotillo canes. A Mexican lad was in charge of the place, but no one was there to meet her. When she mentioned the Martins, the boy pointed to some tents in the distant foothills to the southeast. He indicated he had delivered water to them that morning, but shook his head "no" when she asked him to take her there. The stage driver explained she should now continue to Harrisburg where someone could be found to take her to the Martin's Camp.

Pete's Well was a change station, and the fresh team of horses trotted forth with such speed that, Laura wrote, "I bounced up and down over the rough hilly road, sometimes hitting the canvas overhead, but managing, always, to come down on the wagon seat."[44]

In Harrisburg, Laura was advised to wait in the boarding house, across the street from the general store and post office, until John Agard could finish sorting the mail. He had promised to take her to the mine. Within a few minutes, Rube Martin came into Harrisburg astride Barney. He immediately made arrangements to leave the mule, rented a buggy, and took Laura to Martin's Camp. The letter she had written to her friends announcing her impending visit had arrived on the same stage with her.

One of the three tents became Laura's quarters. She described it as being pitched over a wall of boards three feet high. There was a screen door that had a canvas curtain for privacy, and the door was set into a casing at the lowest part. When she learned this precaution was intended to prevent snakes from invading her tent, she was careful to keep it in place. The tent was divided with curtains to form a living room separate from the bedroom. A kerosene lamp provided light at night.

Water was expensive, costing 50 cents a barrel, at the mine. Although there was always plenty to drink and to use in cooking, Laura was intrigued by their early and creative use of recycling. Water from the wash pan was saved in buckets, carried to the mine, and used for hand drilling. The Saturday night bath water often doubled as water to clean soiled clothing worn in the mine, and dishwater kept special plants and vines growing, adding color to the mountainside camp.

During the long afternoons, Laura sometimes rode Barney over mountain trails. Many hours were spent in quiet talk with Sadie, while Gladys and Marcella romped and played in their rocky yard.

One day, Mary Reid walked from her ranch to visit the Martins. Before the sun had slipped too low in the west, she began her five-mile hike home. Laura rode Barney part of the way on the return trip to keep Mrs. Reid company.

Intent as the men were in mining, they took time off occasionally for recreation. One day all of them picnicked at the Socorro Mine. Another day John hired a team and lumber wagon from Harrisburg, to take Sadie, Laura, Gladys and Marcella to Harqua Hala to see the old mine.

Laura wrote of the many pleasures of her autumn visit at Martin Camp. "September is a beautiful month on the Arizona desert.

The days are warm and sunny…the nights cool and invigorating."[45] She saw a full moon rise above the mountains and watched its slow ascent into the zenith. The moon's eerie light gradually outlined the landscape with a mysterious silver glow. On quiet evenings they all gathered outside the tents, sometimes listening to the night voices on the desert and sometimes singing along with Rube's banjo.

There was one afternoon toward the end of her visit that Laura recalled vividly. Rube let her ride Barney while he followed, walking and swinging his prospector's hammer. Wherever Rube went, he carried the hammer and whacked at outcroppings of rock, for he could not give up his prospector-dream of chipping away a bit of stone to find a bonanza. She and Rube climbed to the top of a mountain where

The Martin family and friends on a picnic near the Reid Ranch.

they had a wonderful view of the surrounding valleys and encircling hills. They watched the sun go down and when the last bright glow had faded, started back to camp. In the distance a great campfire was burning brightly. John Martin was getting ready to prepare his "Arizona frijoles" for Laura.

When the time came to leave, Laura insisted on riding Barney to Pete's Well to catch the stage. With her luggage and a canteen full of water, she climbed up on Barney. They left for Pete's Well in the starlight of early dawn, with Laura riding and John walking beside her. Laura boarded the stage at sun-up.

As the horses plodded along the long road to Congress, Laura reviewed her recent visit in Martin Camp, at the San Marcos Mine. Life in a mining camp, she decided, was no small task for anyone. There was little compensation; there was much hard work, yet no complaints were heard from anyone. She later wrote some of her thoughts on that trip to her friend, Sadie Martin. "You chose to be with your husband, wherever his work required him to be, but you must have longed for the comforts of the (sic) modern home. John may have had dreams of acquiring influence and power, as he did in later years when his friends sent him to the State Legislature. Rube may have coveted the responsibilities of a City Engineer, which he later assumed in Alhambra, California. But so far as I could see, you were putting forth every effort to develop your mine, and meanwhile living happily..."[46]

* * *

After William S. Moffatt was murdered in August 1900, his nephew came to Harrisburg to settle his affairs. For a time the young man operated the general store, but in 1901 the business was turned over to two elderly gentlemen.

Mining continued at San Marcos until 1902, when Gladys and Marcella needed to go to school. John Martin and his brother Ancil purchased the town of Harrisburg and a new experience for the Martin family began. For the first time in their married life, John and Sadie would be living in town.

Chapter Six

The End of an Era

Harrisburg was not destined to grow into one of Arizona's greatest mining camps. However, for more than two decades it promoted the growth of Northeastern Yuma County, by providing a base for supplies and services, which supported an expanding population. A result of Harrisburg's early success in the mining and milling of gold ore in the Centennial District was the influx of prospectors, some of whom discovered the Harqua Hala gold mine. Without Harrisburg's plentiful water supply, operations at the Harqua Hala Mine could have been seriously impaired. The mill at Harrisburg processed ore from several mines in the late 1800's and early 1900's, including: the Carmelita, Socorro, San Marcos, and the Hercules. Like the Harqua Hala and Golden Eagle Mines, these eventually erected small, but adequate camps and mills of their own, which provided continuing work for residents in the area.

In August 1897, a severe windstorm swept through the town of Harrisburg destroying the homes of Joseph Vickers and O.B. Warner. Several places suffered roof damage including Moffatt's general store, the Post Office, the Socorro Company Office and the residence of

Thomas Bouse. Fortunately, no lives were lost. [47]

When the Martins took over Harrisburg in 1902, the town was in the declining years. Business had slowed down, but the store, saloon, stage office and post office were all still open. There was a boarding house, a schoolhouse, a few homes and some tents near the outside perimeter of the town.

The Martin family pictured in their Harrisburg store.

Across the street from the general store where Mr. Martin worked, a Chinese cook prepared and served meals in the boarding house. The Martins often took meals there. Even in a town as small as Harrisburg, the family found life was entirely different than it had been during their ranching or mining years. Their home was adobe. It had a living room, two bedrooms and a large kitchen. When Laura Rutherford came to teach school in Harrisburg, Mr. Martin partitioned one end of the kitchen off to make a bedroom for Gladys and Marcella, and Miss Rutherford stayed with the Martin family.

The Martin family, friends and Barney.

    They often entertained friends in their home, and Mrs. Martin took an active part in planning social events, some of which were held in the schoolhouse.

    About two miles east of Harrisburg, Mr. and Mrs. James Reid, old friends of the Martins, operated their fine ranch. Reid irrigated large fields that produced excellent crops of potatoes, as well as feed for his cattle. Equidistant between his house and the Nord farm, which joined his property on the west, Reid scooped out an earthen pond. He erected two windmills over twin wells, and prevailing breezes swept across little grey hills to keep the windmills turning. The pond served as storage tank for excess water that could be used for irrigation purposes on windless days. Directly beneath the pipes where water spilled as it was pulled from the well by windmills, Reid anchored oblong halves of a large barrel. They made excellent watering troughs for his cattle. From Reid's ranch, a supply of fresh meat, eggs, and vegetables were sold to boarding houses and families living in the Centennial District.

Not long after the Martin's moved to Harrisburg, excitement began to grow about a railroad scheduled to be constructed from Wickenburg through McMullen Valley and across the desert to Parker, where a bridge would span the Colorado River. From there the line would continue across the California desert to join the main Atchison, Topeka and Santa Fe Railroad near Cadiz, California. The branch line would make travel easier and faster between Arizona and California and it would bring rail transportation to the Centennial District, but it would bypass Harrisburg by five miles. *

A short time before Dick Wick Hall moved to the area from Wickenburg, he attended a Halloween party at the schoolhouse in Harrisburg. In her book <u>My Desert Memories,</u> Sadie Martin described Hall as being so witty that he was the life of their party. That night he quickly earned his reputation as a teller of tall tales among residents of the area.

NOTE * The railroad would travel straight along the desert floor, whereas Harrisburg sat in the foothills.

With Charles Pratt and Ernest Hall, Dick Wick Hall laid out a town site where they were led to believe the railroad would be built. A well was drilled and some buildings were erected. But the railroad survey lines were changed to a half-mile south. The original town site became Grace Valley. Hall and his partners began anew, erecting another town site one half mile south, to be closer to the railroad. They named the new town after Pratt's wife and called it Salome.

Dick Wick Hall's Café and Gas Station.

Word of the new railroad brought many people into the McMullen and Harrisburg Valleys. Land and mines were traded, purchased, and sold. New wells were drilled and new homes erected from lumber.

August Nord, a young man from Sweden, joined three of his brothers who were working in mines in the Centennial District. In the fall of 1905, he traded half-interest in a prospect to George Ward for the adobe cabin and land. August Nord and one of his brothers moved into the little adobe place and began developing the land into a farm. They put down a good well and installed a gasoline engine. In a short time the Nord brothers were growing vegetables, alfalfa and fruit trees. Nord's ranch became a landmark in the valley, and their grove of eucalyptus could be seen for many miles.

The Nord Ranch.

The desert valleys now rang with the sound of stakes being driven into the dry earth, as the route for the railroad was laid out. While the town of Salome was being built, many men made their headquarters in Harrisburg, where food and entertainment were available. The old town blossomed again in a bright, brief spurt of glory, but Harrisburg's future as a town was doomed.

In 1905, the Martins sold or traded all their interests in Harrisburg and became the owners of the Harqua Hala Mine. After the new post office opened in Salome on April 14th, 1905, [48] and with the new Brayton Commercial store nearly ready to open, the Martins decided to do some traveling before settling into their new location at Harqua Hala. The family left on an extended trip to Los Angeles and Chicago, Illinois.

When they returned, they moved into a room adjoining the general store in Harqua Hala, while their home was being completed. Again they took meals at a boarding house.[49]

In 1906, John Martin was elected to serve in the Territorial Legislature. Before leaving to assume his duties, the Martin family moved into the new home he had built at Harqua Hala.

In 1908, John Martin returned to Harqua Hala to live. The mines were leased occasionally, but they were never again as successful as they had once been. Gladys and Marcella went away to high school and college, returning each summer to the desert they loved. When the mine wasn't being worked, John remained as watchman. Of that time, Sadie Martin wrote, "We lived on at the camp…having many disappointments, but much happiness…together. Our new home was comfortable, and we had many good friends."[50]

In August 1919, John and Sadie Martin went to Phoenix to visit Marcella. While there, John became ill with influenza and was never strong enough to return to Harqua Hala to live. They moved to Los Angeles, where John Martin died in July, 1920.

* * *

As the terminus of the Santa Fe Railroad moved ever westward, new towns grew up along the line. One by one, residents began an exodus from Harrisburg. On September 29, 1906, the post office was discontinued and mail was sent to Salome.[51] William Beard* could not adjust to the many new improvements taking place in the Centennial District. The town he helped build was no longer important; the post office he had served at as it's first postmaster was closed, and the home where he had lived with his wife Mary, was lonely.

When Mary Beard died, she was interred in the Harrisburg Cemetery. It was by her side, old Bill told friends, that he wanted to be buried when his time came. William Moffatt's grave was there, and a short distance from him, a polished granite headstone marked the grave of Charles E. Curtis, who had operated the Harris Mill for many years. Beyond Curtis, the stage driver Wes Bigbee, had been buried after his last trip between Harrisburg and Phoenix was over. George Ellsworth was also interred in the Harrisburg Cemetery. No headstone marked his grave, but a fence of wood surrounded it.[52]

Fences began to block off large pieces of land. When the comforting clang of the dinner bell at the boarding house was stilled,

Note* William Beard, a.k.a. "Bill Bear" had been among the original prospectors in the Centennial District and was considered an old timer when the Martins first arrived in the area.

William Beard took to the hills to prospect for extended periods of time. He always returned to Harrisburg, to camp in one of the adobe buildings. In the evening a few old timers shuffled down the empty streets to gather in front of the silent saloon. They still talked enthusiastically about lost mines and told unfounded stories of great gold discoveries. The greatest days of mining lay just ahead.

When they had convinced one another that great wealth still laid out in the hills waiting to be found, they again went their separate ways. But, one by one the old prospectors dropped off, and old Bill wandered eventually from Harrisburg to Quartzsite, and on to Yuma. While in Yuma in 1920, he died and was buried there.

Ten years later, when Sadie Martin learned of his fate, she sought out a way to reunite old Bill with the love of his life, Mary.[53] At about the same time, Jim Edwards, a maintenance foreman for the Arizona Highway Department was renovating some of Arizona's historic sites. At Sadie Martin's urging, Edwards made the restoration of Harrisburg Cemetery one of his crew's projects. In 1935, the cemetery was cleared of debris and gravesites were neatly refurbished. A new fence was built around the perimeter of the old cemetery, and an imposing monument erected near the center. Dedication ceremonies included granting William Beard's wish to be placed beside Mary. His remains were exhumed and brought to Salome, and then down the Buckeye road and through the streets of Harrisburg with its remnants of adobe buildings, old Bill was carried to his final resting place. It was the last known burial in the cemetery at Harrisburg.

William (Bill) Beard, a.k.a. "Bill Bear".

Today, the only evidence that a town named Harrisburg ever existed at the southeast end of Harrisburg Valley is the elegant monument standing in the center of the deteriorating cemetery. A plaque mounted on one side of the monument informs curious readers:

HARRISBURG CEMETERY

In memory of the pioneers who gave their lives to the development of the west.

Cactus Kelli at the Harrisburg Cemetery (circa 1936).

Epilogue

New Beginnings

With the Martins, William Beard and so many other original pioneers gone, new settlers would be the ones who heard the whistle of trains echo through the Harqua Hala Mountains.

Occasionally, the old Harrisburg mill processed ore. Mines were still being worked, and the official designation was still Ellsworth Mining District on mining claims, but for other purposes of reference the names of the new towns were used: Aguila, Wenden, and Salome.

By the time automobiles began to bump along the dusty wagon roads, the valleys around the Harqua Hala Mountains were seldom referred to as the Centennial District. Cattle ranches, farms and businesses were expanding. Change was coming, but at a leisurely pace. A pace that remains characteristic of the way the Valley still is today.

Footnotes

[1] The Arizona Bureau of Mines, bulletin 180, "Mineral and Water Resources of Arizona," (1969), p. 39.

[2] Ibid., pp. 43-44.

[3] Miner, April 4, 1882, p.4

[4] Charles H. Dunning and Peplow, Edward H., Jr., Rocks to Riches, (Phoenix, 1959), p. 99.

[5] Sharlot H. Hall, unpublished manuscript

[6] Record of Mines, Yuma County, Book C, pp. 249 ff.

[7] Record of Mines, Book C, p. 323.

[8] Record of Mines, Book C, p. 340

[9] Theobald, Post Offices, p. 90.

[10] Undated Letter, M. M. Rice, Hayden File, Arizona Historical Society, Tucson

[11] Arizona Enterprise, (Prescott) January 5, 1878

[12] Miner, March 15, 1878

[13] Miner, March 15, 1879

[14] Record of Mines, Book C, p. 272

[15] Oasis, (Nogales), June 21, 1917, p. 3.

[16] Rice, undated letter, in the Hayden File (Carmelita Campbell), Arizona Historical Society, Tucson

[17] Record of Mines, Book E, pp. 84 ff.

[18] Arizona Weekly Journal-Miner. July 18, 1886, p. 3.

[19] Journal-Miner, September 8, 1886, p. 3.

[20] Ibid, September 15, 1886.

[21] Ibid, September 22, 1886

[22] Ibid, February 2, 1887

[23] Ibid,

[24] Theobald's, Post Offices, p. 105

[25] Journal-Miner, February 2, 1887

[26] Private Citizen

[27] Sharlot Hall, unpublished Manuscript, p. n.n.

[28] Ibid

[29] "Harqua Hala Placers", The Arizona Bureau of Mines, bulletin No. 168, (1961), p. 32.

[30] Howland Bancroft, "Reconnaissance of Ore Deposits in Northern Yuma County, Arizona," United States Geological Survey, Bulletin 451, (1911), pp. 110-111.

[31] Ibid

[32] Ibid

[33] The Harqua Hala Gold Mining Company, Limited, Directors' and Mine Manager's Report, for 1893, (September 28, 1894, State

Archives, Phoenix.)

[34] Theobald's <u>Post Offices</u>, p. 104

[35] Bancroft "Ore Deposits in Northern Yuma County"

[36] Harqua Hala Report, September 28, 1894.

[37] Dunning & Peplow, Jr., <u>Rocks to Riches</u>

[38] Yuma County, Arizona, McFarland & Poole, Chicago, 1896

[39] Roscoe G. Wilson, "The Big Surprise at Black Henry's Claim", <u>Arizona</u> Magazine of the Arizona Republic. *Permission granted by author for use of story, by letter dated February 28, 1973.

[40] Sadie E. Martin, <u>My Desert Memories</u>, unpublished manuscript, written in 1939, on file at the Arizona Historical Society, in Tucson, Arizona.

[41] <u>Ibid</u>, p. 48.

[42] Sadie E. Martin, <u>My Desert Memories</u>, pp. 53-54.

[43] Laura I. Lamson, <u>A Visit to Martin Camp</u>. Written at the request of Sadie E. Martin in 1939. (Property of Gladys Martin Krenz, Arcadia, CA, 38 pp.)

[44] <u>Ibid</u>, p. 11.

[45] <u>Ibid</u>, p. 16

[46] <u>Ibid</u>, p. 19-20.

[47] <u>The Arizona Weekly Journal-Miner</u>, September 1, 1887.

[48] Theobald's <u>Post Offices</u>, p. 125.

[49] Martin, <u>Memories</u>, p. 61

[50] <u>Ibid</u>, p. 68

[51] Theobald's, <u>Post Offices</u>, p. 105

[52] Sharlot Hall, unpublished <u>manuscript</u>, Prescott

[53] Pvt. Cit.

Disclaimer: Dates, names, locations and other facts are deemed to be accurate, but not guaranteed. We welcome documented corrections and other input for future projects.

Authors Note

I wish to acknowledge and express my special thanks to Gladys Martin Krenz for all her assistance. Gladys' generosity through the years in her sharing the stories, photographs and memories brought the early years in the Valley, into a sharp but loving focus. A debt of gratitude is due to a lady who shared her memories of a childhood in those mining camps of long ago.

Cactus Kelli

This is the first publication of *THE GREAT ARIZONA OUTBACK Rumor and Innuendo Historical Society*. It begins our effort to achieve one of our founding goals of preserving and disseminating the illustrious and rich history of our beautiful valley.

THE GREAT ARIZONA OUTBACK Rumor and Innuendo Historical Society is a 21st Century organization of volunteers dedicated to the discovery and rescue, promotion and preservation of the history and folklore of the McMullen Valley and surrounding areas.

Our energies and efforts are guided by our abiding respect and ever-growing admiration for the pioneers and miners who came before us and first tried to put down roots in our still untamed desert.

"Knowing where you have come from is important in forming an idea of where you want to go."

Alexander Stille

THE GREAT ARIZONA OUTBACK
Rumor and Innuendo Historical Society
Post Office Box 844
Salome, Arizona 85348
gaohistory@earthlink.net